D1356156

This is a Parragon Book.

© Parragon 1997.

Parragon
13-17 Avonbridge Trading Estate
Atlantic Road, Avonmouth
Bristol, BS11 9QD

Produced by The Templar Company plc,
Pippbrook Mill, London Road, Dorking,
Surrey RH4 1JE

Written by Robert Snedden
Illustrated by Peter Bull Art Studio
Series Designer Mark Summersby

Printed and bound in the UK

ISBN 0 7525 1674 4

# •POND•
# LIFE

P
|| PARRAGON ||

# CONTENTS

# INTRODUCTION

Perhaps the first thing that needs to be done is to define what we actually mean by a pond. This is by no means an easy task. There are a wide variety of wet-land habitats, ranging from bogs and fens to large lakes. Somewhere in between, midway between a puddle and a lake, there is the pond. One rough and ready definition is to call any body of water that is small enough for you to cast a stone from one bank to the other a pond. Or, if you prefer, something less than 50 metres or so across. Another definition is to say that it is a body of water that is shallow enough over its entire area to allow water plants to root. You may even wish to consider a ditch full of muddy water as nothing less than a long, thin pond.

Many ponds are artificial, including the village green pond, the garden pond, ponds that were originally dug to provide drinking water for livestock and those used for raising fish. Natural ponds, because of their shallow nature, are transient and apt to be dried out either by evaporation or by the action of plants over the course of a few hundred years or so.

Now we know what we mean by a pond, what should we expect to find there? Water, unless it is terribly polluted, is an incredibly rich environment, supporting a wide diversity of animal and plant life. Around the edge of the pond there will be concentric rings of different environments, ranging from the boggy wetland at the pond's edge to the drier ground further away.

Some plants and animals are entirely aquatic in their lifestyle, such as duckweed and fish. Others split their lives between water and land, such as bistorts, which can grow on land and water, and amphibians such as frogs, newts and toads. There are also animals that only visit ponds, such as birds and various mammals.

One of the fascination of ponds for many people is that much of the pond life can be collected for more careful study. Sweeping a net through the pondweed is not just for children. Take a white dish with you to tip the contents of the net into. It will make it easier to see what you have caught than upending the contents into a jamjar. Handle your catch with care. Many of the pond creatures are delicate and can be easily injured. Some, such as raft spiders and the larvae of water beetles and dragonflies, might give you a painful nip.

If you do take specimens away with you make sure they are kept cool and that predators are kept apart from other animals. Try to return them to the pond after you've had a good look. Make sure you return your specimens to the pond you took them from. Taking them back to a different pond could be helping to spread disease.

By all means enjoy ponds and their wildlife, but respect them too. In the pages that follow you will find just a few of the fascinating plants and animals that make their homes there.

# PONDWEED & DUCKWEED

The most plentiful of the plants on the surface of the average pond are the pondweeds and duckweeds. Duckweeds may grow in such quantity as to completely cover the surface. These simple plants are little more than a single leaf floating on the surface and a dangling root to absorb nutrients from the water. Duckweed generally indicates a pond in trouble, its water made rich in nutrients by the death and decay of the life in it. Lesser duckweed is illustrated here. The broad-leaved pondweed is particularly common on small ponds around a metre deep, where its flat, leathery leaves may cover the surface. Beneath the water the leaves are longer and more slender and the plant is rooted in the mud. In summer, a spike of tiny drab yellow flowers protrudes above the surface.

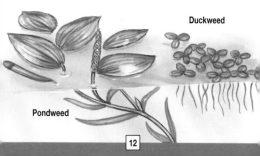

Duckweed

Pondweed

12

# WATER LILIES

Water lilies grow on all types of pond, their roots anchored firmly in the bottom and their large plate-like leaves floating on the surface. The two common British species are easily distinguished, as one has white flowers and the other yellow. The yellow water lily is the more common as its resistance to water acidity allows it to grow in places such as the acid waters of moorland ponds, where the white water lily could not survive. The flower of the white water lily, seen from mid to late summer, is the largest of any wild plant in Britain. The flower stems can be 3 metres in length. The yellow water lily has smaller flowers, but has the biggest leaves of any water plant found in Britain, measuring up to 40cm across. Its flowers appear at the same time as the white water lily's.

# WATER-CROWFOOT

There are several species of water-crowfoot found in Britain, the one illustrated here is the pond water-crowfoot . They are all close relatives of the land-growing buttercups. Crowfoots have masses of tiny green leaves, most of which are generally feathery or needle-like, growing from the stem beneath the water surface. Those leaves that float on the surface are ivy-shaped with three deeply-toothed lobes. Not all species of crowfoot have these floating leaves. Some species of crowfoot are colonisers, appearing only in new ponds, vanishing again after a year or so, while others are common inhabitants of fast-flowing, clear streams and rivers. Crowfoots flower in early summer, when the abundant small white and yellow flowers appear above the surface of ponds and canals.

# COMMON WATER-STARWORT

The starworts are common aquatic plants that are found growing in a variety of locations in ponds and ditches everywhere. There are several very similar species, which can be difficult to separate from each other as there is a great deal of variation within each species. The common water-starwort is shown here. It is just as likely to creep out on to and root on the mud around a pond or stream, as to be found growing floating in the deeper waters. The shape of the leaves depends on whether or not they are submerged, those under water being somewhat long and narrow, while those above the surface are round, forming a rosette at the tip of the shoot. The flowers, which can appear any time from spring to autumn, are tiny and green with no petals.

# WATER-PLANTAIN

The water-plantain is an attractive plant that is commonly found in the shallow water and muddy ground at the edge of ponds and slow-moving rivers. It is absent from the most northerly parts of Britain. Water-plantain is a large plant, growing up to a metre tall, with a cluster of broad, lance-shaped leaves surrounding the base of the slender stem. In summer, tall, branching flower stems appear, with an abundant display of small, three-petalled, pink and white flowers. The flowers only open in the afternoon and each one rarely lasts longer than a day. Each flower produces tiny droplets of nectar, attracting insects and ensuring that the flowers are pollinated.

# AMPHIBIOUS BISTORT

As the name might suggest, the amphibious bistort is just as at home out of the water as in it. In fact, there are two distinct types of this plant. Those growing on land at the water's edge are fairly erect plants. They have hairy leaves, which are green or reddish in colour and grow from the main stem on short stalks. The aquatic form, on the other hand, grows in still or slow-moving water, mostly submerged but with long-stalked, hairless leaves that trail along the water, floating on the surface. Both forms of amphibious bistort can grow up to about 75cm in length and are able to put down roots from anywhere along the stem. The pink flowers, which appear between July and September, grow in short, dense spikes on the end of the flower stalks.

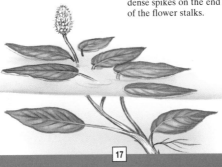

# BLADDERWORTS

There are three species of bladderwort in Britain, all of them rare. The most common, the greater bladderwort, is shown here. These are fascinating plants, whose attractive display of yellow flowers above water gives no indication of what is happening beneath the surface. Bladderworts catch mosquito larvae and other small water creatures in tiny bladders attached to their leaves. If the animal brushes against the hairs at the entrance of the bladder, a trapdoor closes, trapping the animal. The bladderwort absorbs minerals from its decomposing victim, providing it with a supplement to the poor nutrients in the ponds of its heathland habitat.

# WATER-PARSNIPS

The water-parsnips are members of the Umbellifers, a group of plants that includes carrots and parsley. They can be identified by their flowerheads, which are broad and umbrella-shaped clusters of tiny white flowers. Water-parsnips are mainly found growing on the damp ground by the edge of ponds, although on occasion they will also grow in shallow water. The lesser water parsnip (not shown) can be identified by its long-stalked, coarsely-toothed, bluish-green leaves. It may be erect or creeping. The greater water-parsnip, shown here, can grow up to 2 metres tall and has particularly large flower clusters. The leaves are divided into as many as 12 leaflets. The poisonous hemlock water-dropwort (not shown) can be distinguished by its triangular, heavily-toothed leaflets.

# YELLOW LOOSESTRIFE

Yellow loosestrife is a tall plant that is found, often growing in large groups, in damp places such as riverbanks, fens and lake margins, as well as around ponds. It is common in much of Britain, although it is absent from the north of Scotland. Yellow loosestrife reaches a height of between 60 and 150cm. The stems are upright and hairy and the leaves are long and pointed, growing either in pairs or whorls of three or four around the stem. The leaves are blue-green on the underside and the bright green upper surfaces are dotted with tiny black glands. Flowering occurs between July and August, when the bright yellow flowers grow in clusters in loose branched heads.

# PURPLE LOOSESTRIFE

Purple loosestrife is a beautiful plant that is found in damp places around ponds, riverbanks, lakesides and in fens, often in great abundance. The erect, hairy stem is square in cross section, seldom branched and can grow to a height of between 50 and 150cm. The leaves, which have no stalk, grow in pairs on the upper part of the stem and in threes on the lower part. They are spear-shaped or oval, with the lower leaves generally longer than the higher ones. The reddish-purple, six-petalled flowers are carried in whorls around tall spikes growing at the stem ends. Flowering occurs between June and August. Purple loosestrife is not found in the north of Scotland.

# MARSH YELLOW-CRESS

Marsh yellow-cress is found growing in water meadows and along the banks of ponds and rivers in most areas. It flourishes best in conditions where the ground is flooded in the winter and allowed to dry out during the summer months. It may also establish itself in damp gardens, where it can prove difficult to eradicate. Although it is a relative of the edible water cress, marsh yellow-cress is not itself edible. It is an erect plant with a hollow, red-veined stem, growing to a height of between 25 and 60cm. All of the leaves growing from the bottom of the stem are stalked, whereas those leaves higher up may lack stalks. The base of the leaf stalk wraps half-way around the stem. All of the leaves are deeply-lobed with reddish veins. The small yellow flowers, growing on long spikes, appear between June and September.

# SKULLCAP

Skullcap is found in all areas, growing by streams and ponds and in water meadows and other damp locations. It is an upright plant, reaching a height of between 15 and 50cm. The stem, which is square in cross section, may be branched, although sometimes not. The lance-shaped leaves, growing in pairs either side of the stem, have shallow, rounded teeth. The attractive purple and white flowers appear between June and September, growing where the upper leaves join the stem. The skullcap has a characteristic scale, like a pouch, on the back of the sheath from which the flower grows. Skullcap is well-known as a medicinal plant. It produces an oil called scutellarin, which is used to treat nervous disorders and to ease the symptoms of epilepsy.

# LESSER SPEARWORT

Lesser spearwort is a member of the buttercup family that is typically found in damp places such as the edges of ponds and

in meadows. The hairless stems are reddish in colour and may be upright or creeping, with roots being put down from the creeping stems at intervals. The leaves are much longer and thinner than those of other buttercups and are generally spear-shaped, although some variations can be seen between plants. The upper leaves lack stalks. The glossy yellow flowers, which appear between May and September, are carried either singly or in small clusters of a few blooms at the end of flower stalks. Lesser spearwort produces a sap that can cause severe skin irritations and has been the cause of deaths in cattle and sheep that have eaten the plant.

# BROOKLIME

Brooklime grows in shallow fresh water or in wet mud by the margins of ponds and streams. The stems are hollow and creep along from the base of the plant, putting down new roots in the mud or floating in the water. The leaves are oval or round in shape and slightly fleshy in appearance. They grow in pairs on short stalks on opposite sides of the stem. Both stem and leaves are hairless. The flowering stems are upright, with spikes of up to 30 attractive four-petalled blue flowers growing out from the angle where the leaves join the stem. The upright stems can grow to a height of between 20 and 60cm. Flowering takes place between May and September. The leaves are sometimes used in salads as a substitute for watercress but they may be too sharp-tasting for some palates.

# BLUE WATER SPEEDWELL

The blue water speedwell is one of over 20 species of speedwell that can be found in Britain (the brooklime is another). This is one of the larger varieties, growing to a height of between 20 and 30cm. It is found in or near fresh water, by ponds and the banks of streams. The green hairless stems are thick and branching with the stalkless, lance-shaped leaves growing in pairs on opposite sides. The pale blue flowers are produced on stalks that grow from the angle between the upper leaves and the stem, with flowering taking place between June and August. The name speedwell may have come from a belief in the powers of these plants to cure a variety of illnesses.

# WATER FORGET-ME-NOT

The water forget-me-not is a plant of damp and wet places and so the edges of a pond suit it very well. It has a ridged, hairy stem and can grow to a height of between 15 and 45cm. The base part of the stem creeps along the ground, putting down roots along its length. The leaves are generally oblong in shape with rounded tips, growing out from the stem without stalks. The flowers are delightful, the sky-blue and yellow blooms, each up to a centimetre across, being carried in small clusters at the end of the flowering stalks. The flowers appear all through the summer from May to September. It may be confused with the tufted forget-me-not, the flowers of which are much smaller.

# WATER MINT

Water mint is the most common of all the wild mints. It is found growing in wet places, such as woods, marshes and riverbanks and around ponds. It grows to a height of between 15 and 90cm. Water mint cannot be mistaken for any other pondside plant because it has a similar scent to that of garden mint and will often be detected by its aroma before it is seen. It is likely that it was used as a kitchen herb by the Romans around 2000 years ago. The upright, red-tinged stem of the mint is hairy and often branched. The oval, blunt-toothed leaves, which grow in pairs, either side of the stem, are also hairy. The lilac-pink flowers are carried in two to six densely-packed, rounded clusters which appear towards the stem tips. Flowering occurs between July and October.

# YELLOW IRIS

The yellow iris, or flag iris, is found on wet ground or in shallow water, near rivers, streams and ponds. It also grows in wet woods and marshes and is popular with many gardeners. It is a tall, upright plant that grows to a height of between 40 and 150cm. Both stem and leaves are straight and stiff, growing from a stout underground stem. The blue-green leaves, which have a number of fine veins running along the length, are long and flat, coming to a point at the tip. They grow around the stem, forming a fan at the base of the plant. The leaves are sharp-edged and can cut the careless handler. This, with the shape of the leaves, gives the plant its other common name of sword iris. Two to three impressive yellow flowers, each of which can be up to 10cm across, are carried on a long, flattened stem. The yellow iris flowers between May and July.

# WATER HORSETAIL

The horsetails belong to an ancient group of plants. Their ancestors, tall as trees, existed before the dinosaurs and, transformed by heat and pressure inside the Earth, form a large part of today's coal deposits. The common horsetail, growing on damp ground, is often a pest in gardens. The water horsetail is much smaller than its forebears. It is found on marshy ground and in shallow water, often forming dense beds. The upright stem is hollow and jointed, with small branchlets coming off at the joints, although sometimes the branchlets may be entirely absent. It is not a flowering plant, being related to the ferns. This distinguishes it from the similar marestail, which has softer leaves and small pink flowers.

# BOGBEAN

The bogbean, as the name would suggest, is a water-loving plant, typically found growing in shallow water, such as pools, marshes, fens and at lake margins. It is one of the most attractive of the waterside plants. Creeping stems growing beneath the water can spread the plant along large stretches of the waterside. Upright stems, growing to a height of between 10 and 30cm, carry the leaves above the surface of the water. The leaves are divided into three large, rounded leaflets. The pink and white flowers have fringed, hairy petals and are carried in clusters on long stalks above the water, making an attractive display against the leaves. Flowering occurs between May and July.

# GREAT WILLOWHERB

The great willowherb is a tall and impressive plant that can grow to a height

of between 80 and 150cm. Large stands may be seen growing along the banks of ponds and streams. In Britain, it is absent from the north-west of Scotland. The upright, branching stems are softly hairy. The leaves, which are also hairy, are slightly toothed, narrow and pointed, growing in pairs, one either side of the stem. The deep purple-pink flowers are carried singly on long stalks growing out of the angles where the upper leaves meet the stem. The flowers appear between July and August. After they have been pollinated, a long narrow seed capsule about 6cm long is formed on each flower stalk. This will split open to release numerous downy plumed seeds.

# MARSH MARIGOLD

Marsh marigold, also known in some areas as kingcup, is found growing in marshy ground around the margins of ponds and lakes and often near streams. It does best where there is some shade. Sometimes spreading near ground level, the marsh marigold may also grow erect to a height of 15 to 30cm or taller. It is a fairly stout-stemmed plant with broad, shiny-green, heart-shaped leaves growing on long stalks from the base and stalkless, kidney-shaped leaves growing around the upper stem. The conspicuous yellow flowers, which can sometimes be as much as 5cm across, grow on wide branched heads at the top of the stem and are a common sight in spring and summer.

# GREAT REEDMACE

Owing to a mistake made by a Victorian artist, this plant is also known as the bulrush. In his famous painting 'Moses in the Bulrushes' Sir Lawrence Alma-Tadema depicted the infant Moses afloat in a basket surrounded by this plant. It is a typical plant of the pondside, often found in large stands, growing to well over 2 metres in height. Flowering takes place between June and July. The male and female flowers grow separately on the same plant. The female part is the distinctive sausage shape at the top of the stem, with the thinner and paler male flowerhead forming a feathery plume above the female flowers. The leaves of the reedmace are used for weaving.

# GREAT POND SEDGE

Sedges are grass-like plants, but are distinguished from them by their solid, unjointed stems. The great pond sedge is a common water-side plant that is seen around ponds and slow-moving streams. It grows in large clumps, reaching around 1.5 metres in height. The stiff and robust stem is distinctively three-sided. Flowering occurs between May and June but the flowers are small and inconspicuous, without petals. The male and female flowers grow in separate spikes with up to seven male spikes high up the plant and up to five female spikes lower down. The male spikes are dark brown at first, later becoming yellow as they shed their pollen, and the females are greenish.

# COMMON REED

The common reed is a member of the grass family. Dense clumps of this common plant can be found around lakes, ponds and rivers, as well as in fens and marshes. It is a particularly tall plant, frequently exceeding 3 metres in height. The greyish-green leaves are long, growing up to 60cm, with rough edges, tapering to a fine point. Flowering occurs from late summer to early autumn. The dark purple flowerheads are soft and feathery and made up of a number of spikelets of between two and six flowers. Each spikelet is covered in long hairs. The flowers do not have petals and are pollinated by the wind. The tough stems of the common reed are much in demand for thatching.

# RUSHES

Although similar in appearance, rushes are not related to the grasses. True rushes have spiky, cylindrical leaves, rather than the flat leaves of grasses. The jointed rush, shown on the left, is a widespread member of the family found in wet ground almost everywhere. It grows to about 80cm tall. The dark brown flowers grow in many-branched heads, appearing between June and October. The soft rush on the right is another very common species found in similar habitats to the jointed rush. It reaches around 1.5 metres in height. The brown flowers, which appear between June and August, may be loosely branched or in tight clusters

# PROTOZOA

As well as the life you can see, the average pond is home to a myriad microscopic creatures less than half a millimetre long. Normally invisible to the naked eye, some of these minute species can occur in such profusion that they become visible. Some form colonies that appear like fuzzy white haloes around plants, twigs and other solid objects. Others are like blobs of greenish jelly. Under the microscope, individual protozoa are revealed as beautiful and varied animals, including the shape-changing amoebae. Most consume algae and bacteria near the bottom of the pond.

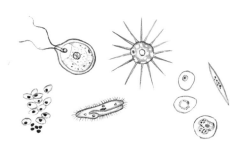

# ROTIFERS

Rotifers are among the larger microbes that can be found in the average pond. The bigger species can reach about 2mm in length, which means that the keen eye may spot them unaided. More than 1000 species of rotifer have been identified so far, and there are doubtless many more still to be discovered. Rotifers are much more complex creatures than the single-celled protozoa and have a number of distinct structures. All of them are predators, sweeping smaller protozoa and other bits of pond debris into their 'mouths' with a fringe of beating hair-like cilia.

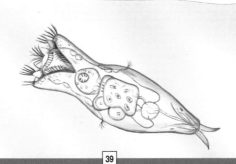

# HYDRA

Hydra are tiny animals related to the jellyfish and sea anemones. They are difficult to find because, like sea anemones, they contract into blobs when disturbed and, in addition, are no more than 15mm long even when fully extended. They are brown or green in colour. The green ones get their colour from colonies of algae living inside them in a mutually beneficial relationship. Hydra have stalk-like bodies, attached by a sucker-like foot to water plants. At the 'head' end there are a number of waving tentacles. These are equipped with poisonous stings, which the hydra uses to ensnare water fleas and other small animals. Hydra reproduce by budding – new animals simply grow out from the older ones, eventually splitting off and becoming independent. Free-swimming larvae, which form new colonies, are produced by sexual reproduction in the autumn.

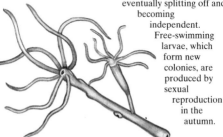

# FLATWORMS

Tiny flatworms, most of which are less than 15mm in length, exist in huge numbers in streams and ponds, gliding over the vegetation and the muddy bottom. There are many different species of flatworm, most of which are black, brown or white in colour. Some are scavengers while others are active hunters, eating water lice and sometimes frogspawn. Flatworms have simple eyes at the head end, but generally find their food by scent. The 'mouth' takes the form of a tube that can be extended from the middle of the flatworm's body. These are the simplest animals to possess a nervous system. A fragment of a flatworm has the ability to regenerate as a whole new worm. Flatworms produce their eggs in the autumn, glueing spherical eggcases about 3mm in diameter to water plants and other solid objects.

# WORMS

Worms can be found in abundance in the mud at the bottom of a pond. Among the smallest are the tiny, threadlike nematodes, less than 5mm in length. Red Tubifex worms are especially common in polluted conditions, as they are adapted to extract oxygen efficiently from poor water. They construct mud-tubes in which they live, sticking out tail first. They form colonies on the bottom of the pond, like fields of red grass. When disturbed, the worms will retreat into their burrows. Ordinary earthworms drown if they are washed into ponds, but there are one or two species that are at home in the water. These include the square-tailed worm, which is found near the banks of ponds and streams. It grows up to 8cm long and is very like an earthworm in appearance.

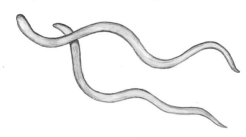

# LEECHES

Leeches are closely related to worms. There are around 20 species in Britain, only one of which, the rare medicinal leech, will even attempt to suck your blood. Most leeches are about 30mm or so in length. Some consume small animals whole, others drain fluids from their prey. One of the larger and more common leeches is the horse leech, which grows to about 6cm in length. Despite its name it does not attack horses, but feeds on smaller animals up to about tadpole size, which it can swallow whole. The medicinal leech is greenish-brown in colour with reddish-orange markings. If there are any in the pond you are exploring they may well come in search of you! If a leech does attach itself do not try to pull it off. It is better by far to let it drop off naturally after it feeds.

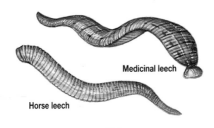

**Medicinal leech**

**Horse leech**

# DAPHNIA

Daphnia, or water fleas, are tiny animals less than 2mm in size, which range from green to reddish-brown in colour. They often become apparent through great numbers, especially in the spring. At this time a population explosion of daphnia feasts on the new season's growth of algae, while they, in turn, become a main food source for fish, frogs, newts and their assorted larvae. These inconspicuous creatures are crustaceans, relatives of the crabs and shrimps. The daphnia's body is folded inside a large plate or carapace, with just its long forked antennae sticking out. It uses these rather than its legs for swimming.

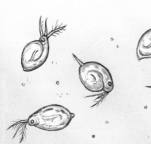

# WATER SNAILS

Water snails live in large numbers in most ponds. They can generally be divided into two groups – the true pondsnails and the ramshorns. Ramshorns are typically like the snail on the left, with a coiled shell, hence the common name. Pondsnail shells are spiral-shaped, reaching a point at the end. Snails vary greatly in size, the largest growing to over 3cm across. Water snails feed mainly on dead plant material and other pond debris, although on occasion they will consume newt eggs. Snails are hermaphrodites, which means that each animal is both male and female. They lay masses of eggs on the leaves of submerged water plants and other objects. The eggs are protected in clear, jelly-like capsules. Snails spend the winter dormant in the mud at the bottom of the pond.

**Pondsnail**

**Ramshorn snail**

# FRESHWATER MUSSELS

Mussels are filter feeders. They suck in water through a siphon, remove any edible particles, and expel what is left out the other side. Large mussels are generally found in deep rivers rather than ponds, but some may be found in larger ponds. The commonest is the swan mussel, which is also the largest mussel found in Britain, with a shell over 20cm in length. Much more common in ponds are the tiny orb mussels and pea mussels. These rarely grow above 1.5cm in diameter. Mussels are most often found in hard-water ponds where there is the calcium they need to build their shells.

# CRAYFISH

Crayfish are particularly sensitive to pollution and are declining in numbers. They are not likely to be found in small ponds in any case, preferring shallow rivers and lakes. Crayfish look like miniature lobsters, of which they are close relatives, growing up to 15cm or so in length. They hide in holes in the bank or under stones by day, taking insect larvae, snails and sick or injured fish in their powerful claws during nightime prowls. The crayfish can use its powerful tail to flip it backwards out of danger. Female crayfish carry their eggs around beneath their bodies. They are said to be 'berried' at this time. After the eggs hatch, the young crayfish may continue to cling to their mother for a time.

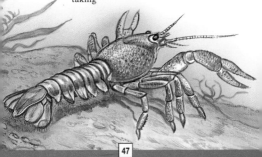

# FRESHWATER SHRIMP

The freshwater shrimp is very much like a miniature version of a marine shrimp in appearance, although it is more closely related to the sandhoppers that can be seen leaping on rotting seaweed at the tideline. The freshwater shrimp is a drab, grey-brown creature, growing to around 2.5cm in length (the females are slightly smaller than the males). It is sensitive to pollution and prefers clean, well-oxygenated water in which to live. Most small ponds are lacking in oxygen and therefore lacking in shrimps as well. It also requires water with a high calcium content, such as would be found in limestone areas, as it requires this mineral to build its shell. Freshwater shrimp are actually responsible for the pink flesh of trout. They are a favourite food of these fish and a pigment contained in the shrimp passes into the trout's flesh. Freshwater shrimps are scavengers feeding on a variety of pond debris, including plant material and dead animals.

# RAFT SPIDER

The raft spider is one of the largest, and also one of the rarest, of Britain's spiders. It is only found around ponds and pools in the more remote fens and marshes. There are in fact two different species of raft spider but they are difficult for any but the expert to tell apart. A fully-grown raft spider can be up to 5cm or more from leg tip to leg tip and it is powerfully built into the bargain. The raft spider tends to lurk around the water's edge or on a floating leaf, or to venture out on to the surface in the manner of a pondskater. It will dive beneath the surface to capture its prey, which may be as big as a stickleback. The female raft spiders carry their eggs around beneath them in slings made of silk, until they hatch and the young spiders become independent. The raft spider is capable of delivering a mildly poisonous bite and it is probably best not to attempt to handle it.

# WATER SPIDER

The water spider spends its life under water. It uses its web, not to catch its prey, but to trap air in a sort of breathing chamber attached to plants beneath the surface. The chamber will also be used as a safe depository for the spider's eggs. Water spiders are fairly widespread and can be found in a variety of ponds. They are around 2.5cm across, legs included. Air is trapped in fine hairs on the spider's body, giving it a silvery appearance as it swims along. Air trapped at the water surface is used to replenish the supply in the breathing chamber. They feed on insect larvae, crustaceans and anything else small enough for them to catch. Water spiders breed in spring, the female guarding the eggs and young carefully until they become independent.

# SPRINGTAILS

Springtails are tiny flight-less insects, rarely more than 5mm in length. They get their name from a forked springing organ at the rear of the insect, which is usually carried folded under the insect's body. If the springtail is disturbed it releases the spring suddenly, propelling itself into the air. Springtails are found in damp, dark places where they feed on vegetation. There are around 300 or so

European species of springtail, of which two of the more common aquatic species are shown here. *Podura aquatica* is less than 2mm in length, and may escape attention on account of its size. It is found in still water, often in large numbers, particularly where duckweed is abundant. *Isotumurus palustris* on the right is a slightly larger species, which may reach 2.5mm in length. Both species are scavengers.

# DAMSELFLIES

Damselflies are most often seen by ponds and streams with plenty of vegetation around the margins. They are very similar to dragonflies in appearance, but they are weak fliers and more delicate. They are easy to distinguish when at rest, as damselflies always fold their wings over their backs, whereas dragonflies hold them open. Like dragonflies, both nymph and adult damselflies are predators, the adults catching flying insects or plucking them from vegetation. Like dragonflies, damselflies mate on the wing and can be seen flying in pairs above ponds in summer. The examples shown here are the common blue damselfly, one of the most common species, and the large red damselfly, which is also widespread.

# DRAGONFLIES

Both water-dwelling nymph and airborne adult dragonflies are voracious predators. The adults live for around a month and are agile fliers, taking their insect prey on the wing. Hawker dragonflies can be recognised by their fast flight, narrow bodies and generally blue and green markings. They are usually found around still waters, but may be seen in towns and along hedgerows far from the nearest pond. The southern hawker is shown here. Skimmer or darter dragonflies are seen over still water, hovering and then darting off suddenly, or sitting on a convenient perch from which to make a swift attack on their prey. The wingspan of the darter is generally greater than its bodylength. The emperor dragonfly, illustrated here, is one of the most impressive of the darters.

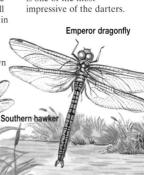

**Emperor dragonfly**

**Southern hawker**

# MAYFLIES

There are over 40 species of mayfly found in Britain. The green drake, or common mayfly, shown here is a large insect, up to 5cm long, more than half of which is taken up by its long three-pronged tail. It can be seen between May and September around rivers and lakes. The greatest part of a mayfly's life is spent as a juvenile. Mayfly nymphs live in the water for up to three years, depending on the species. At the end of this time the nymph emerges from the water at some point during the late spring and early summer months and sheds its skin, becoming a winged subimago. Shortly afterwards the insect moults again to become a fully adult insect, or imago. The emerging insects may form dense swarms above the surface and many are eaten by fish. The adult has no mouthparts and rarely lives more than a day or two. During this time it mates, generally in the evening, and the females lay their eggs on the surface of the water.

# PONDSKATER

The common pondskater is a familiar sight on the surface of just about every pond. It skims or strides over the surface of still waters, using its long middle legs to provide the propulsion and its back legs to steer as it traverses the surface film at high speed. The short front legs are used to catch insects that fall on to the water and the pondskater then uses its long beak to pierce its victim and suck out the juices. It is one of the largest of the surface insects, growing to around 2cm in length. The pondskater is able to fly strongly and will be one of the first insects to colonise a new pond.

# WATER SCORPION

The water scorpion, which is a member of the bug family of insects, spends most of its time beneath the water in shallow, well-vegetated ponds in lowland areas. It does not swim but instead crawls along on the bottom of the pond or hangs just beneath the surface of the water. The water scorpion does have wings and is capable of flying, but it rarely does so. Its brown flattened appearance makes it look rather like a dead leaf, providing it with excellent camouflage. Water scorpions grow to around 3.5cm in length, not including the tail. They feed on insects, tadpoles and sometimes small fish, which they capture in their powerful front limbs. Teeth on the inside of the legs help the insect to grip its prey. The long tail is not a sting but is in fact used for breathing. The water scorpion pushes it through the water surface to take in air.

# WATER BOATMAN

The water bugs are a mixed group of bugs which have adapted to life in the water. Some can spend a greater or lesser time under water, most carrying their air supply trapped in fine hairs or under their forewings, others live on the water surface. Almost all of them are predators. The common water boatman, unlike most other water bugs, such as the water scorpion opposite, is a vegetarian, feeding on microscopic algae and plant debris at the bottom of the ponds it inhabits. They spend a great deal of time grazing on the bottom, rising to the surface to replenish their air supply. The hind legs, which are fringed with hairs, are used for swimming. Water boatmen are also good fliers There are over 30 species of water boatman found in Britain, all of them largely similar in appearance and habits. A few are predatory and some are scavengers, feeding on pond detritus. Male water boatmen 'sing' by rubbing their front legs against a ridge on each side of their face. This is done to attract females during the breeding season.

# WATER CRICKET

Water crickets are not related to true land-dwelling crickets, being so-named because of a superficial resemblance to those insects. They have no call. There are five species of water cricket in Britain and they are very common on ponds and streams everywhere. Water crickets grow to about 0.8cm in length and live on the surface film of the water. They are somewhat similar to pondskaters, but are more stoutly built and can be distinguished by the orange-red marks along their sides. They are generally wingless, although the occasional winged individual may be seen. Water crickets are predators, feeding on insects and other small animals that fall into the water. These are stabbed with the water cricket's long beak, rather than being captured and held by the front legs. In addition, they may also capture mosquito larvae from just beneath the surface.

# ALDER FLY

The alder fly is usually found near still or slow-moving water. The larvae live in water, feeding on a variety of other aquatic creatures. They can often be found underneath stones and other objects on the bottom of the pond. They have seven pairs of feathery gills for breathing under water, which are attached to the abdomen, and a feathery 'tail', which is also a gill. When they are fully-grown, the larvae leave the water and burrow into the soil to pupate, emerging as adults a few weeks later in spring and early summer. The adults scarcely feed at all and they do not live long. The females lay batches of 200 or so eggs on waterside plants where the larvae can fall into the water when they hatch and the insect's life cycle can begin again.

# GREAT DIVING BEETLE

There are many varieties of water beetle. Each carries an air-supply under its elytra, the hardened forewings, when it dives beneath the surface. The hind legs are enlarged to aid swimming, and the insect has a generally streamlined appearance. The great diving beetle is one of the larger water beetles, reaching almost 4cm in length. Both adults and larvae are fierce predators, the adults are strong swimmers and will attack frogs, newts and fish and will even kill the goldfish in a garden pond if they get in. If anything, the larvae, known as water tigers, are even more voracious than the adults. They grow to around 5cm in length. Their hollow, pointed mandibles inject digestive juices into their victims, which are then sucked dry. The great diving beetle's eggs, which are laid in spring, look like tiny white sausages, about 0.5cm in length, and can often be found on the leaves of water plants. There are six species of diving beetle in Britain, all of them largely similar.

# GREAT SILVER BEETLE

The great silver beetle is one of the largest beetles in Europe at around 5cm in length. In Britain it is more or less confined to the south and east of England. It gets its name from the large bubble of air it carries with it under the water, trapped in the fine hairs on its underside. This gives it a silvery appearance. The silver beetles use their antennae to break through the surface to replenish their air supply. The adult great silver is vegetarian, feeding on plant debris in the muddy ponds it inhabits. The larva on the other hand is a fierce predator and can grow up to 7cm in length. It has powerful jaws that are capable of crunching the shells of snails, one of its favourite foods. The eggs are laid in batches of 50 or so, protected inside silken cocoons, which the female leaves floating on the surface of the water. The adult great silver beetle has a sharp spine on the underside of its body that can inflict a painful wound on the careless handler of this water beetle.

# WHIRLIGIG BEETLE

The whirligig beetle is so-called because of the adult beetle's habit of skimming round on the surface of ponds. Around 12 species of whirligig beetle are found in Britain. They may be seen in large numbers, especially in late summer, moving rapidly over the water. The middle and back legs are flattened and covered with hairs, aiding the insect's surface skimming activities. These small, shiny black beetles are about 0.5cm across. They have eyes that are divided into two parts, the upper part for looking over the surface and the lower part for looking under the water. They are predators and scavengers, mostly feeding on insects that fall on to the water. They will dive under water if disturbed. The larvae are also predators. The beetles spend the winter months dormant in the mud at the bottom of the pond, emerging in the spring to lay their eggs on water plants.

# MOSQUITO

Mosquitoes are small, slender-bodied, long-legged flies. The females of many species require a meal of blood to lay fertile eggs and their mouthparts are adapted for piercing the skin and sucking blood from birds and mammals. The males live on nectar and other plant juices. *Culex pipiens* is one of the commonest of the British mosquitoes. The female's preferred victims are birds, rather than humans, although a variety of this insect will readily bite people. It breeds in still water, including garden ponds and rain barrels. The adults hibernate during the winter.

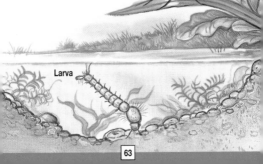

Larva

# CADDIS FLIES

Adult caddis flies are active at night and may sometimes be mistaken for moths. They are brown in appearance, with long antennae and two pairs of hairy wings. Almost all caddis fly larvae live in water and many of these construct cases for themselves from debris. The larvae pupate inside their cases and the adults emerge from the water in early summer.

The larvae are active hunters but the adults scarcely eat at all.

The great red sedge, on the left, is the largest caddis fly to be found in Britain, with a wingspan of 5cm. *Odontocerum albicorne* on the right has exceptionally long antennae, twice the length of its wings.

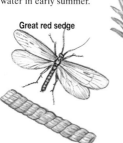

**Great red sedge**

*Odontocerum albicorne*

# PIKE

The largest of Britain's freshwater fish, the pike is a sleek and efficient hunter. An adult female can reach over a metre in length and weigh over 20kg, though the males are much smaller. The long, green-brown body is marked with bronze shading and spots that provide the pike with excellent camouflage as it waits among the water weeds, ready to make a lightning fast strike. Pike usually spawn around February to April. A large female may lay close to half a million eggs, which are attached to plant stems and stones. The larvae hatch after 10 to 15 days, but remain attached to the stems for another 10 days before becoming free-swimming. Large numbers of the young fish die in the competition for food and cannibalism among pike is common.

# STICKLEBACKS

Sticklebacks are found in ponds and streams everywhere and are a favourite catch of children armed with nets and jamjars. The three-spined grows to around 10cm in length and the ten-spined is about half this size. In the spawning season, the male three-spined acquires a bright red throat and belly and blue eyes. He builds a nest on the bottom from plant material and performs a zigzag dance to attract females. The female deposits her eggs inside the nest and the male follows to fertilise them. He will stay to guard both the eggs and the territory around them and tend the fry after they hatch, the only British freshwater fish to do this.

**Three-spined stickleback**

**Ten-spined stickleback**

# COMMON BREAM

The common bream is a bottom-feeding fish found in slow-moving rivers and lakes in lowland districts. It is rarely found north of the Scottish borders. Bream grow up to 80cm in length and may exceed 4.5kg. The young bream is silver, but the adult is bronze with dark fins. It has a deep, flattened body and a relatively small head. The mature fish has a hump, going from the head to the dorsal fin. The spawning season is late spring and early summer, when hundreds of fish form dense, energetic and noisy shoals among the weeds in shallow water during the hours of darkness. A shoal of bream will send bubbling, discoloured water to the surface as they disturb the bottom in their search for food.

# ROACH

The roach is the most widespread of Britain's freshwater fish, being found in fast-running rivers as well as still lakes and ponds. It has a purple-black back, large silvery scales on its flanks and orange-red fins. Juvenile fish or fish in poor condition have pinkish fins. The usual length is around 20cm, but some may reach 35cm or more. Roach usually spawn in May.

At spawning time the eggs are deposited in shallow water, where they stick to water weeds, and hatch about a week later. Young roach may be seen in dense shoals and many will fall victim to pike and other fish. Roach have a varied diet of pondweed, insect larvae, molluscs and crustaceans.

# PERCH

The perch is most often encountered in slow-moving rivers, lakes and ponds in lowland areas. It is absent from the north of Scotland. Perch grow to around 50cm in length and weight about 2kg. The perch is a colourful fish, purple-black on the back, with dark vertical stripes on the flanks and red-tinged fins on the underside.

Spawning takes place between April and June, each female laying up to 200,000 eggs in slow-moving shallow, weedy water. The eggs are laid in strands about a metre long and become entwined in the water weed, hatching 15 to 20 days later. Male perch reach maturity very quickly, sometimes in just six months. The females begin to spawn at around three years old. Young perch eat crustaceans and insect larvae and the adults will also take other fish.

# TENCH

The tench is found throughout Britain, south of the valleys of the Forth and Clyde. A large tench may reach 70cm in length and exceed 2kg in weight. The tench is distinguished by its green-bronze colouring, shading to orange-yellow on the belly. It is a thickset and muscular fish. A short barbel, used for sensing food, hangs from each corner of the mouth. The spawning season occurs during July and August. A large female may lay close to half a million eggs. The fry feed on plankton and algae. Adult tench eat freshwater mussels, snails and other invertebrates. In winter, tench bury themselves in the mud at the bottom of the river or lake at the first sign of frost. They reappear from time to time on warm early spring days.

# CARP

The common carp was originally brought to Europe from Asia by the Romans. Today they are found in warm, shallow waters, such as slow-moving lowland rivers and lakes. Carp may reach a length of about 60cm and a weight of up to 9kg in the wild, domestic fish are bigger. Wild carp are greenish-brown above, shading to yellow below. The mouth has four barbels, one at each corner of the mouth and two shorter ones on the upper lip. The spawning season takes place in early summer. A large female may produce a million eggs, laid among the water weed. The eggs hatch about a week later and the larvae grow rapidly. The adults are bottom feeders, their diet including worms, shellfish and plant material.

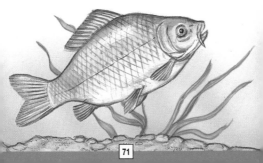

# GREAT CRESTED NEWT

The great crested newt is the biggest of the three species of newt found in Britain, growing to around 15cm in length. It is very dark, almost black, in appearance, with a bright orange or yellow belly. A number of tiny warts cover the skin, hence its other common name of warty newt. In the spring breeding season the male develops the toothed crest that gives the newt its name. It is fairly common and can be found most often in ponds with a good covering of weed, but rarely where there are fish, as the newt tadpoles are apt to be eaten. Great crested newts are strictly protected by law in Britain and it is an offence to catch or harm them.

# COMMON NEWT

The common or smooth newt is found in ponds almost everywhere in lowland areas, although it avoids the acidic ponds typical of heathlands. It is smaller than the great crested, reaching a length of about 10cm on average, and is grey-brown with dark spots and a dull orange belly. Like other newts, it catches its prey with its long sticky tongue, including slugs and worms and other newts if the opportunity presents itself. The common newt breeds in water in the early spring but spends most of its time on land, hiding under stones and logs during the day. Newt tadpoles are similar to the adults, but with feathery gills that allow them to breathe under water.

# COMMON FROG

The common frog varies greatly in colour from grey to orange and red, with speckled markings in red, brown and black. Frogspawn is, of course, something most people associate with ponds. The frogs gather in early spring to breed and lay their eggs in suitable ponds. The tadpoles emerge around two weeks later and reach maturity about three months after that. In early to mid-summer the banks of a pond may swarm with tiny froglets emerging from the water to spend most of their time as adults on the land. Two to three years after they leave it, the adults that have managed to avoid being eaten will return to the pond to breed in their turn.

# COMMON TOAD

Toads prefer deeper ponds than frogs, typically requiring at least a metre of water, but it is not unusual to find both frogs and toads in the same location. Toads do not hop and have a slow, ungainly walk on land. The adult toad is brown in colour with dark spots and is dry and warty to the touch. Toads spend most of their time out of the water, only returning to their ponds to breed. Toads spawn later in the spring than do frogs. The spawning is accompanied by noisy croaking as the males compete for the available females. Toadspawn forms strings, rather than the clumps of frogspawn. Toad tadpoles are jet black in colour, those of frogs are brown specked with gold.

# GRASS SNAKE

Grass snakes are the largest snakes found in Britain and can grow up to 150cm in length, although 90cm is more usual. They are just as likely to be found in fields, marshes or heathlands some distance from the nearest pond. The grass snake is the only reptile in Western Europe that will enter water with any regularity. It is an excellent swimmer and will often go into ponds in search of the amphibians that are its main source of food. The grass snake winds its way sinuously across the surface with its head held up above the water as it searches for its prey. Grass snakes are most commonly encountered around ponds in early summer when the young frogs and toads are emerging.

# GREAT CRESTED GREBE

Grebes are small to medium sized aquatic birds with long, slim necks and dumpy bodies. They are seldom seen on land and are rather clumsy out of the water. They are very much at home on the water, however, and are expert swimmers and divers. The great crested grebe is one of three species found in Britain. It is more likely to be seen on a lake rather than a small pond. In the breeding season, the adults have prominent dark double-crests and a chestnut and black neck ruff. These are used in an elaborate courtship display, that involves much head-shaking and fluffing of feathers. The adults can also be seen presenting water plants to each other as part of the courtship ritual. The nest is made of floating vegetation, such as waterweed and is anchored to reeds. The adults carry the young black-and-white stripe chicks on their backs.

# MUTE SWAN

Swans are the largest of Britain's waterfowl. They are unmistakable, majestic white birds, which swim gracefully on rivers and lakes. On land, they are waddling and ungainly. Once airborne a swan is a magnificent sight, but it does require a long take-off run before it can take flight on its powerful wings. In flight, the wings make a distinctive and evocative throbbing sound. The mute swan is a year-round resident in Britain. At rest, the neck is held in the characteristic curved 'swan-neck' posture. Adults hiss threateningly if annoyed. The nest is a mound of reeds and other plants built near water.

# MALLARD

Ducks are generally smaller birds than geese or swans, with shorter necks and legs. Powerful fliers, they are mainly found on both inland and coastal waters. Male and female ducks generally have distinct plumages, making them easy to tell apart. The duck that is most likely to be seen is the mallard. It can be found in parks and on canals as well as in wilder locations. A pair of mallards may be encountered on even a small pond. Town mallards can be very tame, with an almost dog-like eagerness for food scraps. The breeding male's green head distinguishes it from other waterfowl. The duck has a large blue speculum, the coloured wing patch that distinguishes the females of different duck species. Only the duck mallard utters the characteristic 'quack'.

# MOORHEN

Rails are small to medium-sized ground-dwelling birds that are usually found around ponds, rivers or marshes. They are, on the whole, secretive birds, and are reluctant fliers, preferring to run or swim to escape danger. The moorhen is a typical rail. The white band along the flank and the red forehead are distinguishing features. Out of the water, the green legs may be seen, with a characteristic red 'garter' at the base. The moorhen is found around watersides with plenty of cover along the edges. It is frequently seen in town parks. When disturbed, the moorhen may dive, leaving only its bill above the surface of the water.

# COOT

No other black waterfowl has the white forehead that is the distinguishing feature of the coot. The coot's head and neck are glossier than the rest of the body and the lobed feet, which are unlike those of other rails, can be seen when the bird feeds on land. The coot flies reluctantly, gaining the air with difficulty from the water. It can stay submerged for up to half a minute when feeding. The males are aggressive defenders of their territory, frequently chasing each other off in noisy squabbles. The call of the coot is loud and distinctive, and sounds like 'kook' or 'kewk'.

# HERON

Herons are large wading birds with long necks and legs. They feed in shallow water along the coast or on inland waters or marshes. In flight, the long neck is held hunched up between the shoulders with the legs stretched out behind. Only two species of heron are found in Britain. The bittern (not shown) is a secretive brown bird that skulks in reed beds, fens and swamps. Its booming voice is like a distant foghorn. The grey heron's large size, long legs and snake-like neck make it unmistakable. It is often seen standing still in the water, lying in wait for fish, frogs and other small animals, which it stabs with its long beak before swallowing whole.

# KINGFISHER

The bright blue-green upper parts and contrasting chestnut under parts make the kingfisher one of the most colourful birds of the region. The kingfisher is a medium-sized bird with a long, stout bill and short legs. A swift flier, it may be seen as a sudden, bright blue flash passing along a riverbank. Although it prefers running water, the kingfisher can be found near all kinds of fresh water in lowland areas and will frequently be seen in the vicinity of a pond. The kingfisher will take up position on a suitable perch from which it can keep an eye out for small fish in the water. When it spots its prey, it dives into the water, catching the fish in its beak and bringing it back to the perch to be consumed head first. They make their nests in holes dug into steep riverbanks, both adults sharing in the work of excavating the nest hole.

# WATER VOLE

Water voles are sometimes called water rats, but they are not related to true rats and look quite different, with a flatter face and shorter tail. A large male can be 20cm long, with a tail about half this length. Voles form small colonies, living in burrows in the banks of a pond and it is common to hear them as they plop into the water.

There may be one or two underwater entrances into the voles' network of tunnels. Voles are mainly vegetarian and will stock their burrows with nuts and water plants in preparation for winter shortages. The vole's nest is built from grass deep underground and the females may give birth several times during the summer, usually to twins.

# WATER SHREW

The water shrew is the largest of the three species of shrew found in Britain, with a body length of around 10cm and a tail of similar length. A common mammal, it is occasionally found near ponds and other still water, but its preferred habitat is by running water, where it lives in holes in the river-bank. The snout is long and pointed. The fur on the upper body is grey-brown in colour, while the belly is paler. Shrews are very active, spending much of their time in search of food. Water shrews hunt for worms, tadpoles and insect larvae under water by day and by night. A female may have two broods of five to eight young in the course of the summer. Shrews rarely live much beyond a year.

# BROWN RAT

Brown rats are excellent swimmers and are among the most common mammals likely to be encountered in the vicinity of a pond. This is only because they are so common and adaptable in general – rats are not true specialised pond creatures and will live anywhere they can find food and shelter. Brown rats can be readily distinguished from water voles by their longer ,more pointed snouts and longer tails. A large male rat is bigger than a male water vole, around 28cm with a 20cm tail. Rats breed prolifically, producing several litters during the course of the year. They are not very long lived animals and a two-year-old rat is a rarity.

# OTTER

You would be privileged indeed to live near a pond that was home to an otter. Unfortunately, this fascinating animal has all but disappeared from lowland Britain, although some may still be found in parts of East Anglia. Nowadays, otters are more likely to be seen on the seashores of the west coast of Scotland than paying a visit to the average pond. Now strictly protected by law, the otter may make a comeback to its former territories. The otter's body is long and streamlined for fast swimming pursuit of the fish that are its prey. It has a powerful tail that provides the propulsion.On land it runs in a hunched posture on its short, strong legs. Otters are solitary creatures, males and females only coming together to breed.

# GLOSSARY

**amphibian:** one of a class of animals, such as frogs and newts, that spends part of its life in water as a gill-breathing juvenile and the remainder of its life as an air-breathing adult. All amphibians lay their eggs in water.

**antennae:** the long, often segmented, 'feelers' on the head of an insect or other animal, such as a crayfish or a lobster; a pair of sense organs.

**cilia:** tiny hair-like projections that flick from side to side.

**cocoon:** a silk case made by the larvae of many insects for protection during pupation and also by some adult insects to protect their eggs.

**elytra**: (singular: elytron) the horny, rigid forewings of a beetle that provide a protective covering for the hindwings.

**filter feeder:** an animal, such as a mussel, that obtains its food by straining particles of nutrients from the water in which it lives.

**gills:** the part of a fish, located towards the back of the head, that is used to extract oxygen from the water as the fish breathes, just as an air-breathing animal's lungs take oxygen from the air. The gills have a rich supply of blood vessels into which oxygen is absorbed as the water passes over the gills. Aquatic insect larvae and young amphibians also have gills. Although these have a different structure to those of fish they perform the same function.

**larva:** the earliest stage in the life of many animals, including fish, insects, and amphibians, after hatching from the egg, when it looks different in form and appearance and will generally have a different lifestyle from the adult it will eventually become.

**mandible**: an insect's jaw, which can be of different shapes according to the insect's diet; most flies and butterflies do not have mandibles.

**metamorphosis**: the change that takes place as an insect, amphibian or other animal turns from a larva into an adult, usually while it is resting as a pupa. Complete metamorphosis occurs when the larvae changes form completely, such as a caterpillar turning into a butterfly. Incomplete metamorphosis occurs when the larva more or less resembles the adult to begin with, such as the nymph of a dragonfly.

**nymph**: a young insect that looks similar to the adult, but does not have fully developed wings, for example a dragonfly nymph.

**petals:** inner leaf-like parts of a flower, usually brightly coloured to attract insects that will pollinate the flower. Wind-pollinated and other plants that do not rely on insects tend to have small, inconspicuous flowers.

**plankton:** microscopic living organisms, both plants and animals, that float and drift with the current, rather than moving under their own power, in both marine and fresh water environments.

**predator:** an animal that obtains its food by killing and eating another animal.

**prey:** an animal that is killed and eaten by another animal for food.

**protozoa** (singular protozoan)**:** the simplest forms of animal life, which are microscopically small and consist of just a single cell. Some species of protozoan form colonies of many individuals, which are large enough to be visible to the naked eye.

**pupa**: the stage in the life of many insects when they are changing from larva to adult. At this time the insect does not feed and usually does not move while its body is restructured by the process known as metamophosis into that of the adult insect.

**rostrum**: the beak or snout of a weevil or bug, used for piercing its prey.

**scavenger:** an animal that obtains its food by consuming dead plants or animals.

**species:** an animal or plant of a particular kind that can be distinguished from all other living things. Opposite sex members of a species can breed together to produce a new generation that will be similar in appearance to their parents.

# TITLES IN THIS SERIES INCLUDE:

## ASTRONOMY
## CARD GAMES
## CLANS & TARTANS
## FASTEST CARS
## FLAGS OF THE WORLD
## FRESHWATER FISH
## GARDEN BIRDS
## HANDGUNS & SMALL ARMS
## HISTORIC BRITAIN
## HUMAN BODY
## INSECTS
## INVENTIONS
## MODERN COMBAT AIRCRAFT
## NATURAL DISASTERS
## POND LIFE
## ROCKS & FOSSILS
## WILD FLOWERS
## WORLD WAR II COMBAT AIRCRAFT